Written by Catherine Zoller

Pictures by Mr. Sketches

"Getting these books in people's hands so people's hands pick up The Book."

ABOUT THE AUTHOR

Catherine Zoller is a writer from Tulsa, Oklahoma,
With a husband, three kids and half a college diploma.

Many years ago the Lord impressed her heart one night
Saying simply and clearly, "I want you to write."

So she jumped out of bed and grabbed paper and pen
And waited on the sofa for Him to speak to her again.

At last came the dawn with the dew and the mist,
But all she had written was half a grocery list.

Still she never forgot the words spoken that night;
All she had to learn was that His timing's always right.

Now she's written some rhymes that tell the Bible story
From Genesis to Revelation and reveal God's glory.

The hope in her heart is to show everyone
That reading God's word can be lots of fun.

It will instruct you and teach you and change your heart,
And this little book is designed to help you start!

Revelation: The Rhyme and Reason Series by Catherine Zoller
Copyright ©2015 by Catherine Zoller
Printed in the USA

All rights reserved. This book is protected under the copyright laws of the United States of America. This book may not be copied or reprinted for commercial gain or profit. Reproduction of text, cover, and illustrations in whole or in part without the express written consent of the author or publisher is not permitted.

ISBN 978-0-9885122-2-1
For worldwide distribution

Rhyme & Reason Ministries International • P.O. Box 470994 • Tulsa, OK 74147-0994
You can learn more about Catherine Zoller at www.catherinezoller.com

ABOUT THE ILLUSTRATOR

The artist Mr. Sketches is also known by some
As Mr. David Wilson, and he thinks art is fun!

The nickname Mr. Sketches came from a T.V. show
The station TBN broadcast for three years in a row.

His lovely wife named Karen likes to teach the third grade.
They moved 'round a bit, but when they got to Tulsa stayed.

Art from the heart surely helps God's children to succeed,
So when he draws and sketches, this is always David's creed:

"With broad point or with fine or whatever time or season,
It's time to draw the line now, whatever rhyme or reason!"

DEDICATION

This book is dedicated to Jesus Christ my King,
Whose glory, praise and honor I will forever sing.

He is the risen Savior, the true God's only Son,
Our righteous Redeemer, the Overcoming One.

He sits at God's right hand and rules the universe,
And He will come again and reverse the earth's curse!

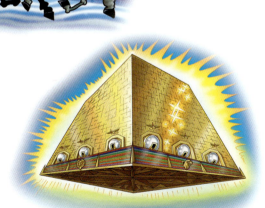

INTROD

"The Revelation of Jesus Christ" is the title of God's book,
It simply means, "revealing" and invites us to take a look

At Christ's ultimate victory o'er Satan, death and sin
When nations finally bow and we all see that Jesus wins!

God's pulling back the curtain of this great mystery,
And giving us a glimpse of the end of history.

As you read remember it was written for a time
When those who stood with Jesus put their lives on the line.

Yet the Word of God is timeless; it's ever and always true,
Applying to each generation, all the way down to you!

There is a war in heaven raging for the hearts of men,
O'er who will have authority to rule them from within.

uction

More like a movie than a book written in a clever way,
It was a style of imagery familiar in that day.

Some things are just symbolic, others taken literally,
Which to the Jewish Christians would make sense immediately.

A storm of persecution was gathering with great force,
And would unleash its fury on those following God's course.

Jesus was saying to His church, whom He holds so dear,
"God's in control of history; you needn't walk in fear."

This book is merely telling the same story again and again,
Each time adding more details to fill the reader in.

And everything He's written must be kept in proper view,
Knowing that He wants it understood by me and you!

The book of Revelation is quite frightening to some.
It tells of what was happening and what was soon to come.

It sent a warning to the church of persecution quite severe
Sweeping through the Roman Empire where Christians lived in fear.

God's promise if we read it is we'll certainly be blessed;
His safeguard and protection will forever give us rest.

Behold! He's coming with the clouds and every eye will see.
Including those who pierced Him through and nailed Him to a tree.

Zech 12:10; John 19:37

"I'm the Alpha and Omega, the first and then the last,
Who was, and is, and is to come!" His voice a trumpet blast.

The book was given by the Spirit to dear John, quite old.
He wrote down everything he saw just like he had been told.

Exiled to rugged Patmos, a Roman island prison,
'Cause he refused to stop preaching the Gospel he'd been given.

Which was that Jesus was the Christ, anointed Son of God,
Who willingly gave up His life to save a world sin-flawed.

Rev. 1:1-9

Caught up in the Spirit, *2 Cor. 12:4*
    he saw many wondrous things:
The glory of our God displayed;
    the wrath on sin He brings.

John turned to see who spoke and saw
    seven golden lampstands,
And in their midst, the Son of Man,
    in white with golden band.

His head and hair were white like wool
    or freshly fallen snow, *Dan. 7:9*
His voice like the rushing waves
    that tumble as they flow. *Ezek. 43:2*
        Dan. 7:13-14; Ezek. 1:28b
His eyes blazed like a flame of fire,
    His feet like polished brass, *Dan. 10:6*
And His strong face shown as brightly
    as sparkling, gleaming glass.

His right hand cradled seven stars,
    the elders of each church.
From His mouth, a two-edged sword,
    'tween joints and marrow search.
        Heb. 4:12-13

Then John collapsed as one who'd died
    but heard, "Don't be afraid!
At one time I was dead
    and in a tomb where I'd been laid,

To the seven ancient churches,
  John wrote each a letter,
Stating what they had done well,
  and what they could do better.

First, the church of EPHESUS, 1
  the Lord thought fairly well of,
Yet He warned them quite sternly
  that they had left their first love.

To the church of SMYRNA, 2
  "I know your works and poverty,
But if you're faithful unto death,
  you'll live and reign with Me."

And to the church at PERGAMUM, 3
  there is both bad and good.
Faithful in a hostile place,
  but not shunning things they should.

To the church of THYATIRA, 4
  He told of their good deeds,
Yet said they were corrupted by
  the men who would mislead.

The SARDIS 5 church He found was dead
  in sin and in decay,
And they were warned quite sternly
  they must turn, repent, obey.

Rev. 2:1-3:13

The church at PHILADELPHIA?
  He found no fault in them.
They had all been faithful to His word
  and they worshipped Him.

And last, to LAODICEA,
  it seemed they could do more.
Their lukewarm attitude revealed
  that though rich, they were poor.

'Cause they were neither hot nor cold
  He vomited them out.
He begged them to repent of sin
  and turn their lives about.

Christ then said, "I'll come in and dine
  with those who are My own."
Those who overcome will sit
  with Christ who is enthroned.

While each church mentioned did exist
  in times so far away,
The warnings must be heeded still
  by churches of today.
  Rev. 22:5; 2 Tim. 2:11-12
The promise then and now to those
  who overcome and pray,
Is we'll reign with Him in Heaven
  one bright and glorious day!
  Rev. 3:14-22

A voice said, "Come up here and see the things which soon take place. And John was shown events within this marvelous age of grace.
I Thes. 4:13-18

As John looked up he saw a door in heaven opened wide. All the glorious things inside, he tried hard to describe.
Rev. 4:1

HEAVEN'S EYE VIEW
REV. CHAPTERS 4-11

God Himself sat upon His throne where He forever rules. *Isa. 6:1*
And John describes the scene for us by using precious jewels.
Ezek. 1:26-28

He saw four and twenty elders who
   were clothed in pure white robes,
All adorned in golden crowns,
   'midst thunderous lightning strobes.

Before the mighty throne of God
   the seven lamps were lit;
The seven lamps of fire to show
   the fullness of His Spirit. *Isa. 11:2*

With mighty peals of thunder *Ex. 19:16*
   and a sea like crystal glass,
There came four awesome creatures
   with their eyes in front and back.
Rev. 4:2-6

The first was like a lion,
  the next a newborn calf. *Ez. 1:5-14*
If you could see them worshipping
  you might with great joy laugh!

Third, a face just like a man,
  then an eagle high in flight;
Each of them before the Lord
  would worship day and night.

For evermore their job is
  to sing out His praises rightly,
"Holy, holy, holy, is
  the Lord God, the Almighty,
    Isa. 6:3

"Who was, who is, who is to come on back to earth again!"
The elders sitting 'round the throne, fell down and worshipped Him,

Declaring that His great power created all we see,
And by His will it all exists, including you and me! *Col. 1:16-17; Rev. 4:7-11*

John sees in the right hand of Him
   who sits upon the throne,
A holy scroll with seven seals
   that's waiting to be shown.

It is the title deed to Earth
   that Jesus had created;
Legal papers Satan stole,
   that's kept us separated. *Gen. 3:1-7*

He heard a mighty angel with
   a voice of grave appeal,
Shout out, "Who is worthy here
   to open up these seals?"

But there was no one qualified.
   John wept and was undone.
If no one worthy could be found,
   Earth's redemption couldn't come.

An elder then stepped forward saying,
   "Do not yet despair,
Behold the Lion of the tribe
   of Judah is right there!" *Gen. 49:9-10*

John turned and saw a Lamb that looked
   as if it had been slain; *Ex. 12:21*
The Lamb who died at Passover
   to take our sin and pain. *Jn. 1:29; Rev. 5:1-6*

The Lamb then took the scroll from Him
who sits upon the throne.
For only One is worthy—
the Savior who claims His own.

Our Jesus is the Root and Branch,
the Lion and the Lamb,
The King of Kings, our great High Priest,
who is both God and man.

Among the elders and creatures a new song now was sung,
Declaring God redeems the folks of every tribe and tongue.

Then angels by ten thousands joined to sing a song of praise
To Jesus, perfect Lamb of God, who from the grave did raise.
Lk. 24:1-7

And so all those in heaven, and down on the earth below,
Will declare those things forever that all of heaven knows.
Phil. 2:9-11

Blessing, glory, honor, power belong to Him alone.
To the righteous Lamb of God who sits upon His golden throne!
Rev. 5:7-14

So when the first seal was opened, John heard a voice say, "Come!"
He looked to see a pure white horse whose hooves beat like a drum.

Upon it was a rider with no sword, but with a bow.
He rode forth, come for conquering, so that much we do know.

When the second seal was broken, John saw a horse fire red,
Who took peace from the earth and filled the people's hearts with dread.

At the breaking of the third seal, a black horse and rider
Were sent to the earth to bring severe hardship upon her.

The fourth seal brought another horse whose rider's name was Death,
Who from a fourth of humankind then stole their living breath.

Rev. 6:1-8

When the fifth seal next was split,
   all who'd died for His name's sake
From underneath the altar cried,
   "How long Lord must we wait, Rev. 4:2, 8:3

"For You to get revenge on those
   who took away our lives?"
God is just. Men will be judged
   for evil ways and lies. Deut. 32:35

Then they were given robes of white
   and told, "Not very long."
When their number was complete,
   God would right what had been wrong.

When the sixth seal was broken, lo!
   there was a mighty quake. Joel 2:10-11
The sun turned black, the moon like blood,
   let there be no mistake. Isa. 10-11, 19

Tumbling stars fell to the earth.
   Skies rolled up like a scroll. Isa. 34:4
Mountains and islands shifted place.
   The earth moved as a whole.

Then whether rich or poor, they hid;
   whether a slave or free.
Every unbeliever cried,
   "Let mountains fall on me!
Rev. 6:9-17

"Just hide us from the anger
    of the righteous, Holy Lamb,
For His fierce wrath has come at last,
    and now no one can stand!"

But to everyone who loves the Lord
    with all his heart and soul, *Deut. 6:5; Lk. 10:27*
We'll all rejoice to see the world's
    redemption as foretold.

Then John beheld four angels
    at each corner of the earth.
Who were supposed to judge the folks
    without a second birth. *Jn. 3:3-6*

No wind did blow upon the earth,
    the sea nor any tree.
An angel sent from the Lord spoke
    saying, "Listen now to me!

"Do not yet harm the earth nor fill
    the people there with dread,
'Til we have sealed the bondservants
    with marks on their foreheads."

The mark upon their forehead
    gave the angels all the nod.
The saints would be protected
    by our great and loving God.

John heard the number that was sealed from every tribe of Jews.
From every camp of Israel 12,000 God did choose.

The total then, from every tribe, those chosen to be sealed,
144,000, just as the Lord revealed.

Rev. 7:1-8

Then John saw a multitude from all nations, tribes, and lands
Clothed in purest white with palm branches in their hands.

They cried, "Salvation belongs to our God and to the Lamb!"
And worshipped at the feet of Him who is the great "I AM."

Ex. 3:14

The angels 'round the throne, the elders and living creatures,
Fell down and worshipped God and all His marvelous features.

Saying, "Blessing, glory, honor,
   to our great God above,
Thanksgiving, wisdom, power and might,"
   to the Lord of love.

An elder asked, "Who are these
   who sing in adoration?"
"They are those who came out
   of the great tribulation."

They've washed their garments in His blood,
   they serve Him night and day
In the heavenly temple,
   and He wipes their tears away.

Now came the time to break the last seal numbered seven.
For half an hour it was silent everywhere in heaven.

Next John saw seven angels receiving seven trumpets,
Thus begins the unleashing of the seven trumpet judgments.

Rev. 7:9-8:4

Another angle came out
  with a censer of incense,
And he added it to prayers
  of saints who took a stance.

The angel took the censer
  filled with fire from the altar,
And threw it down to earth
  which began to shake and falter.

Thunder roared and lightning flashed
  and there were earthquakes too.
The seven angels raised their trumpets
  high and then they blew.
              Rev. 8:5

At the fourth, a third of all
the heavenly lights went black.
An angel flew through mid-heaven
to sound the last attack.

The fifth horn sounds, a star falls,
Satan rises from the pit.
The Destroyer came with locusts;
the wicked must submit.

John heard a voice from the altar
at the sixth trumpet's blast.
"Release the four strong angels
who were bound up in the past." Jude 6

So those who had been prepared
for that hour, month and year,
Came forth to torment all mankind
and fill their hearts with fear. Rom. 2:5-6
2 Tim. 3:1-5

Remember now, my dear ones,
that God's wrath is not for you!
He'll save all of His children but
judge those whose hearts aren't true.
Rev. 8:12-9:16

John saw a mighty angel with a small book in his hand,
Who had his right foot on the sea, his left one on the land.

Clothed in a cloud and with a shining rainbow 'round his head,
And when he spoke the seven thunders bellowed out and said,

"Seal up these things which you are told and do not write them down!"
John stopped what he was doing, laid his stylus on the ground.

The angel raised his hand and made an oath to God above,
Who made the heavens and the earth because of His great love.

The angel cried that there should be
   no longer a delay,
For God to judge a nation
   that would soon be wiped away.

Then the angel told old John
   a strange and curious thing,
"Eat the scroll and prophesy
   of nations, peoples and kings."

At that point John was given
   a reed like a measuring rod,
And told to measure the temple
   of our majestic God.

But he was not to measure
   the court outside the temple.
Because for forty-two long months,
   the Gentiles would it trample.

Da. 7:25; 12:7
Rev. 10:1-11

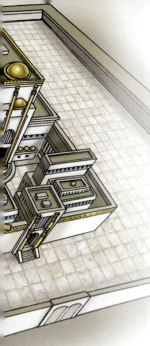

And during all this time, two witnesses will be God's voice,
Crying out for sinful people to make a different choice.

They will be given power from on high to prophesy,
And to shut the heavens up so no rain falls from the sky. *I Kings 17:1*

The beast will then ascend from the bottomless pit below,
And make war against these two men, and strike a deadly blow.

For three and one half days they will lie dead in that foul city,
And there's no doubt at all that the picture won't be pretty.

Yet people will rejoice when they see that these men are dead,
'Cause they refused to honor all the words the men had said.

But after three and one half days
   they will rise up and stand,
When God breathes air into their lungs,
   they live at His command!

He takes them into heaven where
   they'll reign evermore.
And quakes will shake the earth
   just like they had before.

A tenth of the city falls,
   the rest fills with fear and awe,
And so out of their terror
   they will give glory to God.
Rev. 11:1-13

7 When the sounding blasted forth
from angel number seven,
Loud and righteous voices could be
heard throughout all heaven.

The twenty-four elders worshipped Him upon the throne,
For judging all the wicked and rewarding His own.

They'll declare the kingdoms of this world have been undone.
Finally now, at long last, our God's Kingdom reign has come!

The temple was reopened, the covenant ark was seen,
And all the celebration made for quite an awesome scene!

This scene always reminds us that God's word is just and true,
And hearkens to the covenant He made for all of you. *Gen. 9:9; I Kings 8:9; Gen. 12:1-3; Acts 3:24-25 Rev. 11:15-19*

nd then John saw a woman representing Israel,
With whom the covenant of old remains and always will.

The woman there was pregnant and cried out in labor pain.
We're told the child is Jesus who would come but not yet reign.
Isa. 66:7

He saw a great red dragon with seven heads and ten horns,
Ready to devour the Child as soon as He was born.

Satan knew which nation would bring Messiah to the earth,
So patiently he waited to destroy Him at His birth. Gen. 3:15
Rev. 12:1-5

For he hates the living Savior,
   the One he tried to kill, Matt. 2:16
From long before His birth,
   all the way to Calvary's hill. John 19:30

But when God creates a holy plan,
   He surely sees it through;
And somehow makes a way to do
   the things He wants to do.

Yet Satan roams about the earth
   seeking people to devour. 1 Pet. 5:8
But because of Jesus Christ
   the victory now is ours! 1 Pet. 5:9

For we can overcome him by
   the blood of Christ the Lamb,
And our testimony spoken
   throughout all the land.

Then John beheld a horrid beast
   come rising from the sea. Isa. 57:20
The dragon gave it power, strength,
   and great authority.

It had ten horns and seven heads,
   on each head was a crown, Dan. 7:7-27
Which represent the earthly kings
   and kingdoms all around.

Across the seven heads was written
   a blasphemous name.
Speaking out against our God,
   denying His right to reign.
          Rev. 12:7-12; 13:1-2

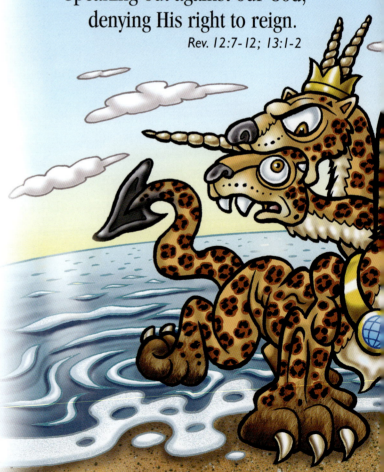

And all the world bowed down
    before the dragon and the beast.
Apparently no one's conscience
    was bothered in the least.

The wicked people turned their backs
    on our great God above,
To reject His open arms
    reaching out to them in love.

And then one of the heads received
    a blow that should sure kill.
When he appeared to have been healed,
    they bowed down to him still.

A phony resurrection meant
    to mimic the Messiah's,
Will seem at last to finally give
    the devil his desires.

Satan will at last get what
    he's wanted all along,
Which was to get the high praise
    that alone to God belongs. Matt. 4:10

And all whose names aren't written down
    in the Lamb's book of life,
Will bow before the dragon and
    still live in sin and strife.

Rev. 13:3-2

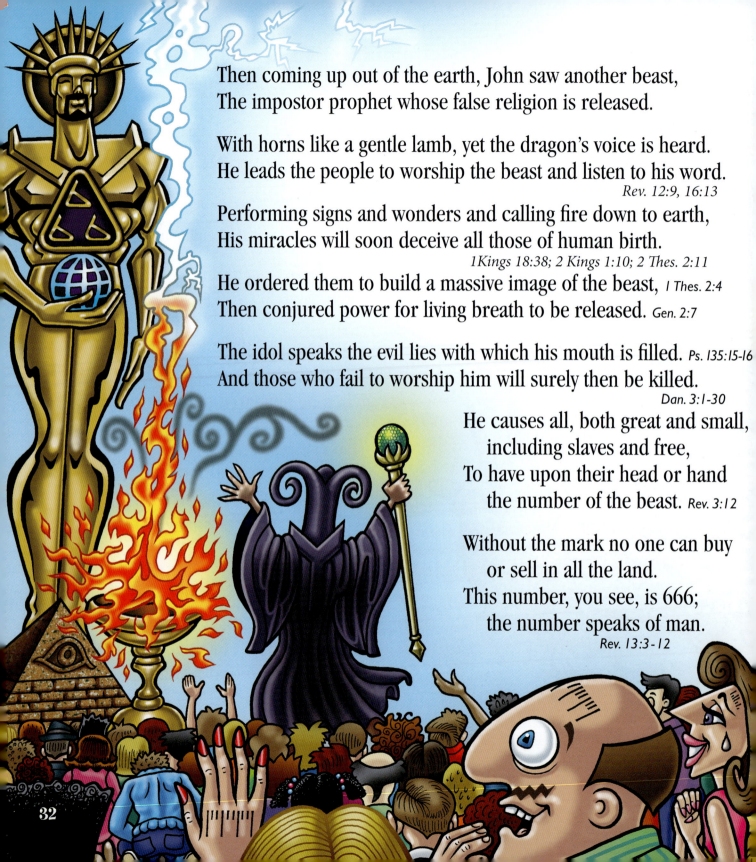

Then coming up out of the earth, John saw another beast,
The impostor prophet whose false religion is released.

With horns like a gentle lamb, yet the dragon's voice is heard.
He leads the people to worship the beast and listen to his word.
Rev. 12:9, 16:13

Performing signs and wonders and calling fire down to earth,
His miracles will soon deceive all those of human birth.
1Kings 18:38; 2 Kings 1:10; 2 Thes. 2:11

He ordered them to build a massive image of the beast, *I Thes. 2:4*
Then conjured power for living breath to be released. *Gen. 2:7*

The idol speaks the evil lies with which his mouth is filled. *Ps. 135:15-16*
And those who fail to worship him will surely then be killed.
Dan. 3:1-30

He causes all, both great and small,
including slaves and free,
To have upon their head or hand
the number of the beast. *Rev. 3:12*

Without the mark no one can buy
or sell in all the land.
This number, you see, is 666;
the number speaks of man.
Rev. 13:3-12

ohn leaves the tribulation scene and the events in heaven,
The 144,000 written down in Chapter 7,

Were standing on Mount Zion with the Lamb of then and now.
And they all had His Father's name penned across their brow.

They sang a new song before
 the creatures, elders, and throne.
The only ones who knew the song
 were the redeemed alone.

Rev. 14:1-5

John looked and saw an angel
   flying by in heaven's midst
With an eternal Gospel for
   every tribe, tongue on the list.

Crying out with booming voice,
   "Fear God and give Him glory,
The hour of His judgment comes."
   And things will now get gory.

The Gospel message is the same
   as it's been all along,
Salvation comes to those with faith,
   but wrath for choosing wrong.

All those who bow down to the beast
   are warned then by the call,
To worship Jesus Christ alone
   before the nations fall.

A second angel spoke the doom
   of wicked Babylon.
A third one cried a warning that
   was heard by dear old John.

"Those who bow down to the beast
   will drink the wine of God's great wrath." *1 Tim. 5:24*
God in His grace and mercy
   warns us to avoid that path. *Rom. 10:13*

Then John heard a voice from heaven say,
   "Blessed are those who die
In the Lord from now on!" *Ps. 116:15*
   And he heard the Spirit cry,

"They may rest from their labors,
   for their deeds follow with them."
For we will *all* give account
   the day we stand before Him.
      2 Tim. 4:8; Col. 3:23-25; 2 Cor. 5:10;
      Rev. 14:6-13

Then John looked and saw
   the Son of Man sitting on a cloud;
In His hand a sharp sickle,
   and an angel cried out loud,

"Thrust in Your sickle! Reap the harvest!
   Now the time has come!"
The earth was ripe, He thrust it in,
   and then the deed was done.

The nations who reject the Lord
   are depicted as a vine.
The clusters from the vine of the earth
   are pressed like bitter wine.

John saw another sign in heaven,
   great and marvelous.
A sea of glass mixed with fire,
   and those victorious,

Who did not worship the beast or the number of his name.
They sang the song of Moses. Heaven filled with its refrain.
   Rev. 14:14-15:4

Next John saw the tabernacle
in heaven opened wide.
To the seven angels, "Pour out
your bowls on every side."

The temple filled with smoke
to show the glory of our God.
No one else could enter
'til the angels did their job.

As each angel poured out his bowl,
God's righteous judgments came.
Yet men refused to quit their sin,
and cursed His holy name.
Jn. 3:19-20

And with the seventh judgment,
as the earth shook violently,
The great empire of Babylon
split into parts of three.

Every island fled away and
the mountains were not found.
And huge hailstones fell from the sky
that weighed a hundred pounds.
Rev. 15:5-16:21

GONE IS BABYLON!

John saw another angel there
  with great authority,
Cry, "Fallen now is Babylon,
  no more a great city."

He called her many sins aloud,
  her shameful, wicked state.
Another voice from heaven warned
  not to participate.

Out of God's love for His people,
  He summons them to leave,
To escape the sinful city and
  the plagues due on that eve.

And all who prospered from her
  will lament her fiery end.
The swiftness of her doom
  takes just an hour to descend.

For like a giant boulder
  that is thrown into the sea,
She'll be destroyed forever,
  finished to the last degree.

Rev. 18:1-19:2

The troubling ends to make way
  for Christ's presence to return.
The seven years are over
  and a fourfold praise begun!

John heard the chorus above the earth
  sing praises with a nod,
"Hallelujah! Power! Glory!
  And Salvation to our God!

REV. CHAPTERS 19-20 — EL SHADDAI EYE VIEW

"Because His righteous judgments are forever true and right."
And so the throng in heaven sang to God with all their might.

He judged the city Babylon who corrupted all the earth,
To avenge the blood of martyrs who'd had the second birth.

The elders and living creatures all fell prostrate on their own,
Saying, "Hallelujah!" to our God who sits upon the throne.

Again John heard the choir sing,
"Rejoice and give God glory!"
Our marriage to the Lamb becomes
the best part of the story.

"The Bride," who are the saints of God,
"has gotten herself ready."
(To think about Christ as our groom
is really very heady!)

She was given a bridal gown
of linen clean and bright.
In contrast to the scarlet city,
she's clothed in purest white.

The costly linen represents
the righteous acts of man.
"Blessed are those invited
to the marriage of the Lamb."

2 Cor.5:21; Jas. 2:26;
Rev. 18:3-9

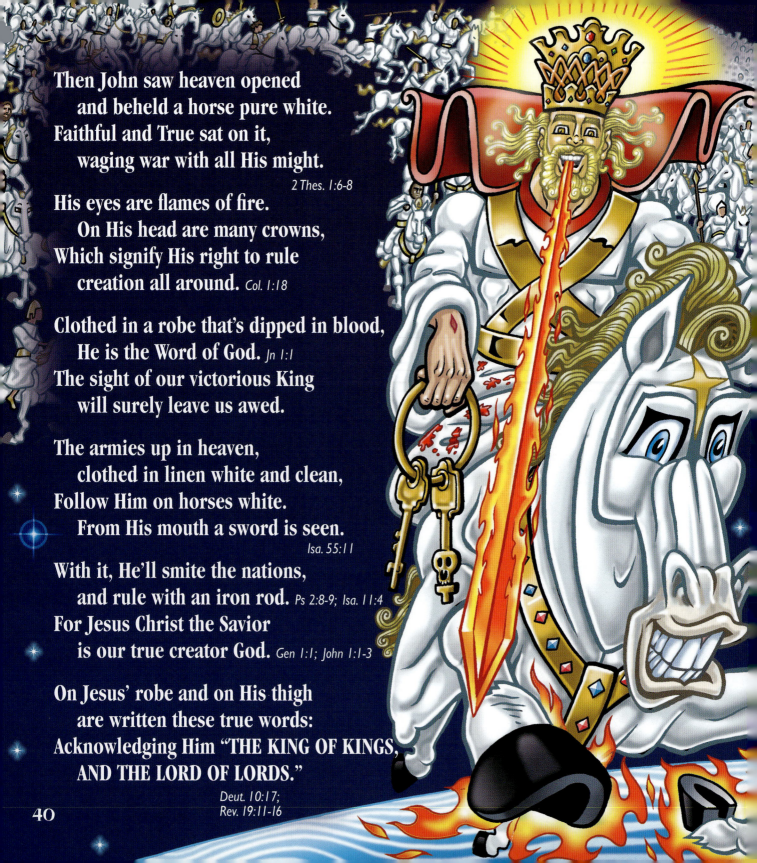

Then John saw heaven opened
 and beheld a horse pure white.
Faithful and True sat on it,
 waging war with all His might. 2 Thes. 1:6-8

His eyes are flames of fire.
 On His head are many crowns,
Which signify His right to rule
 creation all around. Col. 1:18

Clothed in a robe that's dipped in blood,
 He is the Word of God. Jn 1:1
The sight of our victorious King
 will surely leave us awed.

The armies up in heaven,
 clothed in linen white and clean,
Follow Him on horses white.
 From His mouth a sword is seen. Isa. 55:11
With it, He'll smite the nations,
 and rule with an iron rod. Ps 2:8-9; Isa. 11:4
For Jesus Christ the Savior
 is our true creator God. Gen 1:1; John 1:1-3

On Jesus' robe and on His thigh
 are written these true words:
Acknowledging Him "THE KING OF KINGS,
 AND THE LORD OF LORDS."

Deut. 10:17;
Rev. 19:11-16

And then John heard an angel cry
 to raptors in the sky,
"Come and eat the flesh of all
 those who are to die."

Those fiends who joined the evil one
 to shed the blood of saints,
Will die when they make war with Him
 who never sleeps nor faints.

The beast was seized and with him,
 the false prophet who deceives;
Thrown down into the lake of fire
 from which there's no reprieve.

And all of Satan's armies were
 soon slaughtered by the sword,
Which came from out of Jesus' mouth,
 our overcoming Lord!

John saw an angel come from heaven
 with a key and chain,
To throw the dragon into the pit,
 a thousand years restrained.

Matt. 25:41

And so the dragon, ancient foe,
 the serpent known of old,
No longer fools the nations.
 He has finally lost his hold.

Rev. 19:17-20:3

The tribulation martyrs,
  with no mark on head nor hand,
Will sit on thrones and judge with Him
  who now rules in the land.

After one thousand years the dragon
  will be freed awhile.
Once again that old liar
  will deceive folks and smile.

He'll talk them into waging war
  with legions millions strong.
But heaven's fire will then descend
  to crush the evil throng.

Satan himself will be thrown down
  into the lake of fire.
The beast and false prophet
  will burn forever with that liar.
    Rev. 20:4-10

John saw a great white throne with all the dead both small and great,
Standing there before the Judge to hear their endless fate. Jn. 5:22; 2 Tim. 4:1

The sea gives up its dead, as well as Hades and each grave,
Each person will be judged by deeds, and whether they are saved.

For those not found in The Book of Life, their situation's dire.
Along with death and Hades, they'll be thrown into the fire.
Matt. 7:13-14; 1 Cor. 15:54-55; Rev. 20:11-15

Then heaven and earth will pass away, the sea will be no more.
The new Jerusalem will come down like a bride adorned.
2 Pet. 3:13

A voice cried out, "God's tabernacle resides on earth with men,
And they shall be His people, and He shall dwell with them.

He'll wipe away each pain filled tear and He will say no more
Will there be death nor crying; no pain nor reason to mourn."

He who sits upon the throne exclaims,
 "All things I will make new!"
He said to John, "Write! My words
 are faithful, good, and true." Rom. 8:19-22

Again He said, "It's done.
 I'm the beginning and the end,
To him who thirsts, the springs
 of living water I will send.

"And he who overcomes will now
 inherit all these things.
I will be his God forever,
 and over him I'll sing. Zeph. 3:17

"But all the unbelievers
 I will cast them from my sight.
The second death, the lake of fire,
 will be the sinners plight."
Jn. 5:29; Ro. 6:23;
Rev. 21:1-8

REV. CHAPTERS 21-22 — ETERNAL EYE VIEW

One of the seven angels said,
"Come here and see the bride,
The wife of the Lamb of God,
who'll rule now by His side."

John went in the Spirit
to a mountain high and great.
And saw the holy city
with it's twelve imposing gates.

Her brilliance is like a costly stone
of jasper, crystal clear.
And I will tell you this, young friends,
there's nothing like it here!

With three gates built on every side:
north, south, east and west.
On twelve foundations, names of
the apostles who were blessed.

An angel measured the city off.
It was a perfect cube.
It shimmers with fine jewels and gold.
You'll want to see it too!

Each gate was made with just one pearl, the streets were paved in gold;
And all of these foundation gems are wondrous to behold!

Rev. 21:9-21

There is no temple in this place,
    nor is there moon nor sun.
God and Lamb are the temple
    and the light there is the Son!

The gates will never have to close.
    The night will be no more.
No sin nor anything unclean
    will plague us like before.

The river of life, crystal clear,
    will flow down from the throne.
On each side stands a tree of life,
    complete and fully grown.

Each and ev'ry month they'll bear
    a different kind of fruit.
Its leaves will heal the nations,
    and all curses are now moot.

At last the curse is gone,
    and we shall finally see His face!
On our foreheads is His name,
    and we'll praise Him for His grace!

Shekinah glory from our God
    is the only light we'll need.
As we rule and reign with Him,
    we will worship at His feet.

Rev. 21:22-22:5

The thirsty ones can come
and drink from the river of life.
And God, Himself, will gladly grant
them all eternal life.

The One who testifies these things
says, "I am coming soon."
So live your life in harmony
with Him to be in tune.

I hope to see you all there!
Jesus wishes none to die.
All you have to do, my friends,
is invite Him to live inside!

Rev. 22:18-21